Y0-AEA-216
3650 Summit Boulevard
West Palm Beach, FL 33406-4198

FAIRY TALE PHONICS

THEO SWIMS WITH A MERMAID
A TALE OF CONSONANT SOUNDS

by Rebecca Donnelly
illustrated by Carissa Harris

GRASSHOPPER

Tools for Parents & Teachers

Grasshopper Books enhance imagination and introduce the earliest readers to fiction with fun storylines and illustrations. The easy-to-read text supports early reading experiences with repetitive sentence patterns and sight words.

Before Reading
- Discuss the cover illustration. What do readers see?
- Look at the picture glossary together. Discuss the words.

Read the Book
- Read the book to the child, or have him or her read independently.
- "Walk" through the book and look at the illustrations. Who is the main character? What is happening in the story?

After Reading
- Prompt the child to think more. Ask: Look around you. What objects have consonant blends in their names? What objects have digraphs? Sound out and spell each word.

Grasshopper Books are published by Jump!
5357 Penn Avenue South
Minneapolis, MN 55419
www.jumplibrary.com

Copyright © 2023 Jump! International copyright reserved in all countries. No part of this book may be reproduced in any form without written permission from the publisher.

Library of Congress Cataloging-in-Publication Data

Names: Donnelly, Rebecca, author.
Harris, Carissa, illustrator.
Title: Theo swims with a mermaid: a tale of consonant sounds / by Rebecca Donnelly; illustrated by Carissa Harris.
Description: Minneapolis, MN: Jump!, Inc., [2023]
Series: Fairy tale phonics | Includes index.
Audience: Ages 5-8.
Identifiers: LCCN 2022030006 (print)
LCCN 2022030007 (ebook)
ISBN 9798885242783 (hardcover)
ISBN 9798885242790 (paperback)
ISBN 9798885242806 (ebook)
Subjects: LCSH: Readers (Primary)
LCGFT: Readers (Publications)
Classification: LCC PE1119.2 .D678 2023 (print)
LCC PE1119.2 (ebook)
DDC 428.6/2–dc23/eng/20220719
LC record available at https://lccn.loc.gov/2022030006
LC ebook record available at https://lccn.loc.gov/2022030007

Editor: Eliza Leahy
Direction and Layout: Anna Peterson
Illustrator: Carissa Harris

Printed in the United States of America at Corporate Graphics in North Mankato, Minnesota.

Table of Contents

A Splash by the Shore	4
Let's Review!	22
Picture Glossary	23
Index	24
To Learn More	24

In This Book:

You will find consonant blends and digraphs. A consonant blend is two consonants next to each other, like "**fl**-". Each letter makes its own sound. A digraph is two consonants put together to make one sound, like "**th**-". Can you find the consonant blends and digraphs on each page?

Hint: Examples of consonant blends are **fl**ing, **sw**im, and **st**ory. Examples of digraphs are **th**ink, **sh**ark, and **wh**iz. See if you can spot them!

A Splash by the Shore

Theo is at the beach.

He swims near the shore.

He sees a splash!

"Who is there?" asks Theo.

He searches behind a rock.

He checks below the surface.

He catches a glimpse of a mermaid!

"Whoa!" says Theo. "What are the chances?"

"Hi!" says the mermaid. "I'm Philippa."

7

"How do you swim?" Theo asks.

"With a swish of my tail," Philippa answers.

She swims in circles around Theo.

"I'm searching for a special shell," says Philippa. "Do you think you could help me?"

"Without a doubt!" says Theo.

"This way!" says Philippa.

"Shh!" says Philippa. "A shark!"

The shark shows its shiny teeth.

Theo shivers.

Swish!

The shark dashes after a fish.

fish

Theo and Philippa whiz through the water.

They see a giant tail.

"Whose tail is that?" asks Theo.

Whoosh!

The whale's tail whips.

"Whoa!" says Theo.

tail

"Phew!" says Philippa. "Look, three dolphins! What are they playing with?"

"It's a shell!" shouts Theo.

"My special shell!" says Philippa.

shell

Theo floats toward the dolphins.

"Can my friend please have that shell?" he asks.

"Yes!" says one dolphin.

The dolphin flings the shell into the air.

It flies over Theo.

Philippa catches it.

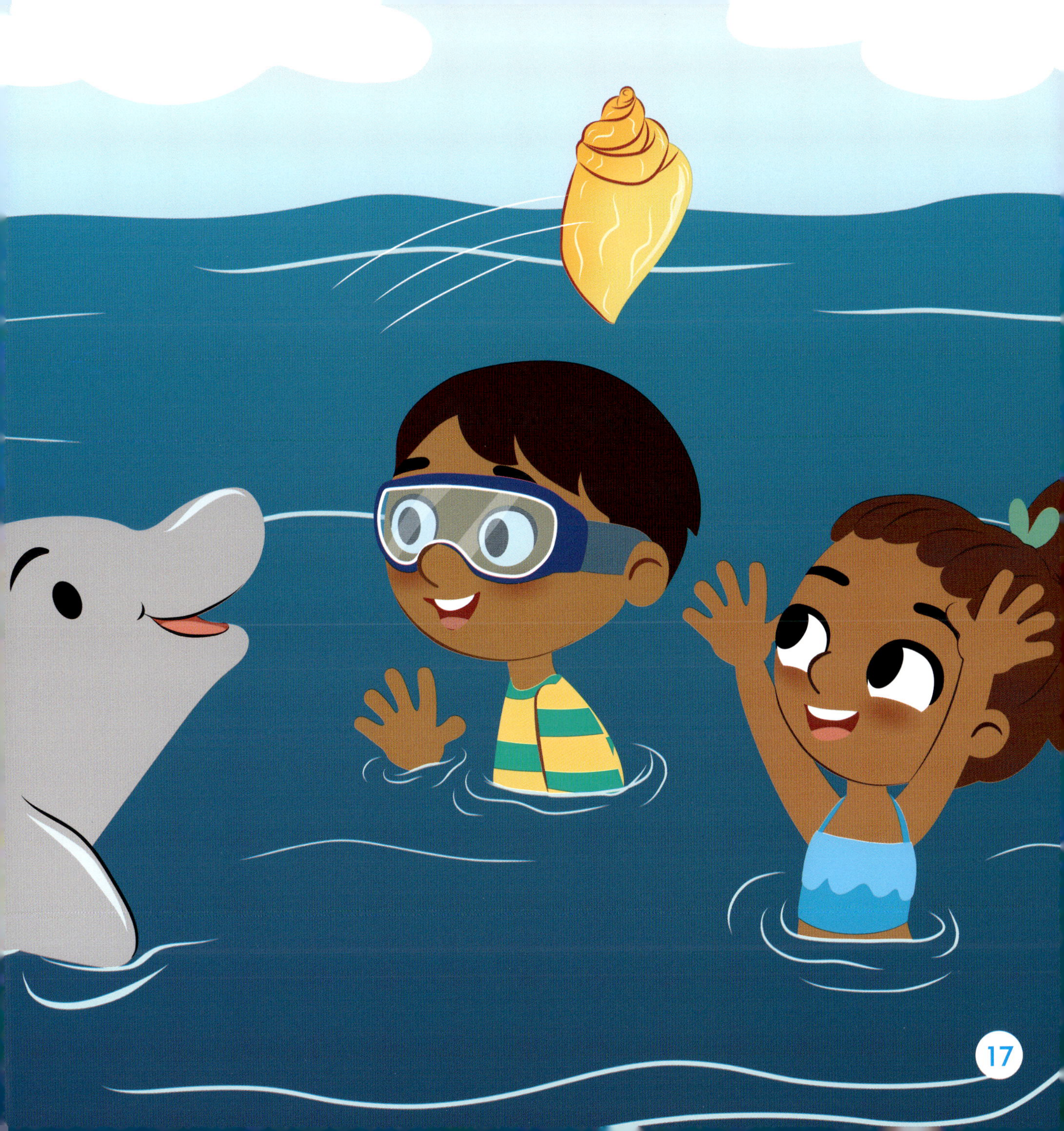

"This is a secret gift for my friend," says Philippa. "Come with me!"

Philippa and Theo swim to Philippa's home.

A crab crouches by her door.

"Crawl inside this shell!" says Philippa to the crab.

19

"I should go home, too," says Theo. "My stepdad is waiting for me."

"I see him standing on the shore," says Philippa.

"I can't wait to tell him this story!" Theo says. "Goodbye!"

"Goodbye!" says Philippa.

21

Let's Review!

A digraph is two consonants put together to make one sound, like **ch**- and **ph**-. In a consonant blend, each letter makes its own sound, like **cr**- and **sw**-. Which words below have digraphs? Which have consonant blends? Sound out each word to help.

whale

teeth

stepdad

shell

beach

crab

rock

swim

dolphin

Picture Glossary

crouches
Bends one's legs and lowers one's body.

flings
Throws something with force.

glimpse
A quick or partial view.

mermaid
An imaginary sea creature with a woman's head and upper body and a fish's tail instead of legs.

surface
The top or outermost layer of something.

whiz
To move very quickly.

Index

beach 4

catches 6, 16

crab 18

dolphins 14, 16

fish 10

flings 16

floats 16

mermaid 6

rock 5

searches 5, 9

shark 10

shell 9, 14, 16, 18

shore 4, 20

splash 4

swims 4, 8, 18

tail 8, 12, 13

teeth 10

whale 13

To Learn More

Finding more information is as easy as 1, 2, 3.

❶ Go to www.factsurfer.com

❷ Enter "**Theoswimswithamermaid**" into the search box.

❸ Choose your book to see a list of websites.